volume **4**

BIG BIRD'S
SESAME STREET
DICTIONARY

FEATURING JIM HENSON'S SESAME STREET MUPPETS

LETTERS H–K

by Linda Hayward

illustrated by Joe Mathieu

Editor in Chief: Sharon Lerner

Art Directors: Grace Clarke and Cathy Goldsmith
with special thanks to Judith M. Leary

Funk & Wagnalls, Inc./Children's Television Workshop

Hh

A B C D E F G **H** I J K L M N O P Q R S T U V W X Y Z

hair Hair grows on the top of your head and on other parts of your body. Look up the word body.

> My **hair** is long and straight.

> My **hair** is short and curly.

> Animal **hair** is sometimes called fur...

> ...or wool.

half A half is one of two equal parts. The two parts together make a whole thing.

> Zounds! **Half** of the pie is missing!

hammer A hammer is a tool for hitting nails and other things.

Prairie Dawn is building a tree house. She is using a **hammer** to pound a nail into the wood.

hand Your hand is the part of your body at the end of your arm. Look up the word body.

Prairie Dawn is holding a **hammer** in her **hand**.

NAILS

handle   The handle of something is the part that you hold on to.

Biff's lunchbox has a **handle**.

Sully's hammer has a **handle**.

handsome   When something is handsome, it is nice to look at.

> I think my snuffle is very **handsome**.

hang   To hang means to be attached to something above.

Betty Lou can **hang** by her knees.

When you hang on, you hold tightly.

> **Hang** on, Tessie!

happen
When something happens, it takes place.

> Why do these things always **happen** to me?

happy   When you are happy, you feel good about things.

The Count is **happy**.

> 1...2... 3...4... four bats. Ha, ha, ha... I love to count bats.

hard   When something is hard, you cannot easily change its shape. When something feels hard, it does not feel soft.

> Ouch! This rock is **hard**.

> A sheep's wool is soft.

hard   When something is hard to do, it takes extra work or special skill. It is not easy to do.

> It's easy to make cookies.

> But it's **hard** to wait while they bake.

hat   A hat is something that you wear on your head.

hatch   When baby animals hatch, they come out of eggs.

Farmer Grover **had** six eggs.
Now he **has** six chicks.

have   When you have something, it belongs to you.

have   Have also means to be holding or keeping something for someone else.

hay   Hay is a kind of grass that has been cut and dried. Cows and horses eat hay.

Farley dropped his sewing needle in a pile of **hay.**

he   He is another way to say man or boy or male animal.

Sherlock Hemlock is looking for a needle in a haystack. Do you think that **he** will find it?

head   Your head is the part of your body above your neck. Look up the word body.

Bert has a pot on his **head.**

healthy   When you are healthy, you feel well and your body works the way it should.

> I do exercises to stay **healthy.**

hear   You use your ears to hear sounds.

Super Grover has super **hearing.**

> I, Super Grover, can **hear** the sound of a cookie jar being opened in the next room.

heart   Your heart is inside your chest. It pumps blood to all parts of your body. Look up the word blood.

The doctor is listening to Betty Lou's **heart.** She can hear it with her stethoscope.

> A **heart** is also a special shape.

heavy Something that is heavy is harder to lift than something that is light.

Say, Ernie, why is it that I am carrying the piano and you are carrying the piano stool?

Gee, Bert. I thought the piano *and* the piano stool would be too **heavy** for you.

heel Your heel is the back part of your foot. Look up the word body.

height The height of something is how tall or high it is.

The Count is measuring Big Bird's **height** from his **heel** to the top of his head.

242... 243...244... two hundred and forty-four centimeters! That is ninety-six inches.

8 ft.

heel

helicopter A helicopter is a flying machine with a large propeller on top. Helicopters can fly in any direction.

Granny Fanny Nesselrode is flying in her **helicopter**. She can see the tops of the buildings.

hello Hello is something you usually say when you greet someone.

What do you say when you meet a two-headed monster?

Hello. Hello.

What's new?

How are you?

How to say hello around the world

helmet   A helmet is a hard hat that is used to protect the head.

Super Grover wears a **helmet**.

help   When you help someone, you find ways to make things easier or nicer for that person.

Super Grover likes to **help**.

When I put on my **helmet**, I change into brave and fearless... SUPER GROVER! Now I must find someone who needs my **help**.

hen   A hen is a female chicken. Some other female birds are also called hens.

Super Grover saw a **hen**.

This is boring sitting here all day keeping these eggs warm. I could use some **help**.

her   Her is another way to say woman or girl or female animal. It can also mean belonging to a woman, a girl, or a female animal.

The hen was tired of sitting on **her** eggs. Super Grover wanted to help **her**.

There is someone who needs my **help**. Down, down, and away!

HELP! HELP!

here   Here means in this place.

Here is a picture of Super Grover and the hen.

Get out of **here**, you...you... you furry blue thing!

Oh, do not thank me! I am happy to **help**. We super**heroes** live to serve.

hero   A hero is someone who is brave and fearless and very helpful.

Super Grover thinks he is a **hero**.

THE END

hide When you hide, you stay where no one can see you. When you hide something, you put it where no one can find it.

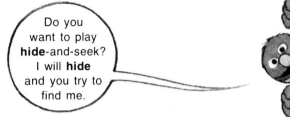

Do you want to play **hide**-and-seek? I will **hide** and you try to find me.

high Something that is high is farther up than something that is low.

I can reach the **high** shelf.

I can reach the low shelf.

hill A hill is a small mountain.

Prairie Dawn is climbing up the **hill.**

him Him is another way to say man or boy or male animal.

Herry Monster lost his doll. Betty Lou returned it to **him.**

hip Your hips are on both sides of your body below your waist. Look up the word body.

Prairie Dawn is dancing with her hands on her **hips.**

hippopotamus A hippopotamus is a big animal with a large head, short legs, and thick skin. It lives in a river or a lake.

Behold the **hippopotamus**! He is heavier than the lot of us!

his His means belonging to a man, a boy, or a male animal.

Ernie is holding **his** bat.

hit When you hit something, you strike it.

Ernie is going to **hit** the ball with **his** bat.

hold When you hold something, you take it in your hands.

Marshal Grover has to **hold** on to Fred's tail so he won't fall off.

hold   Hold also means to keep something in place. Containers can hold many different things.

This box can **hold** my collection of bottle caps.

hole   A hole is an opening in something.

Super Grover has a **hole** in his cape.

holiday   A holiday is a special day in the year when people celebrate something. On some holidays people do not work or go to school.

The Fourth of July is a **holiday.** On the Fourth of July we celebrate the birthday of the United States.

home   Your home is the place where you live.

Ernie and Bert's **home** is in an apartment house.

Big Bird's **home** is a nest.

This is my home

mobile home

castle

farmhouse

igloo

cave

beaver dam

birdhouse

log cabin

lighthouse

apartment house

trash can

honey   Honey is a sweet syrup made by bees.

The queen is in the parlor eating bread and **honey.**

Me love **honey.**

The SESAME STREET PLAYERS

HONEY

hook   A hook is used to hold things, catch things, or fasten things. A hook is bent at one end.

Can you find three kinds of **hooks** in this picture?

hop   When you hop, you jump up and down.

Grover loves to **hop.** He is playing **hop**scotch.

Do you see how I am **hopping** from square number one to square number two?

HOME 7 6 5 4 3 2 1

horn   A horn is a musical instrument that you blow into.

horn   A horn is also something that makes a loud noise to warn people.

horn   The horns on the heads of some animals are made of bone or hair and are used for protection.

I, the Amazing Mumford, will now pull from this perfectly empty hat three different things with the same name.

A LA PEANUT BUTTER SANDWICHES!

Now where is that other kind of **horn**?

It's right behind you, Mumphie!

horse

A horse is an animal with four long legs, a mane, and a tail. People can ride on horses.

I am a baby **horse.** I am a foal.

I am the foal's mother. I am a mare.

Whoa, Fred!

I am the foal's father. I am a stallion.

Some **horses** can run very fast.

hospital

A hospital is a building where people go when they need special help from doctors.

I'm in the **hospital** because the doctor took out my tonsils.

hot

When something is hot, it is very, very warm.

Oh! This porridge is **hot!**

What a **hot** day!

THE SESAME STREET PLAYERS

GOLDILOCKS AND THE 3 BEARS

hotel

A hotel is a building where people pay money to sleep and eat when they are away from home.

Granny Fanny Nesselrode is going to stay at the Sesame Gulch **Hotel.**

SGH

SESAME GULCH HOTEL

CABLE T.V.

hour

An hour is an amount of time. An hour is sixty minutes long.

Hey, Bert. It takes one **hour** for my pet fish to swim a hundred laps.

Are you through with the bathtub, Ernie?

Hour by hour with Ernie and Bert

Time to get up

Breakfast time

Playtime

Lunchtime

Clean-up time

Dinner time

Bath time

Bedtime.
Good night!

house A house is a building to live in. Some houses are big enough for only one family. Apartment houses are big enough for many families.

I live in a **house.**

I live in an apartment **house.**

I live in a bird**house.**

how How means in what way or in this way.

Can you tell me **how** to get to Sesame Street?

Sure. Follow that bird.

hug When you hug someone, you put your arms around that person.

huge When something is huge, it is very, very big.

Snuffle-upagus is too **huge** to **hug.**

hundred One hundred is a number. One hundred is one more than ninety-nine.

There are one **hundred** cents in a dollar.

97...98... 99...100... one **hundred** cents! Wonderful!

hungry When you feel hungry, you want to eat.

Biff and Sully are **hungry.** They are having lunch.

hunt When you hunt for something, you look for it.

hurry When you hurry, you move faster than usual.

Sherlock, I lost Rubber Duckie.

Please **hurry**, Sherlock. I can't take my bath without Rubber Duckie.

Have no fear. I, Sherlock Hemlock, the world's greatest detective, will **hunt** for it.

hurt When you hurt, you feel pain.

Frazzle bumped his foot. His foot **hurts.**

husband A husband is a man who is married.

I am married to him. He's my **husband.**

I am married to her. She's my wife.

This dictionary has left out a good H word— heap!

Some of my favorite heaps are junk heaps, garbage heaps, and rubbish heaps.

I i

A B C D E F G H **I** J K L M N O P Q R S T U V W X Y Z

I I is a word you use when you are talking or thinking about yourself.

ice Ice is frozen water.

Herry Monster is skating on the **ice**.

I like to skate on the **ice**.

I think he should be more careful.

I think this **ice** is cold.

ice cream Ice cream is a sweet, frozen food made with cream and sugar.

idea An idea is a thought in someone's mind.

Now, what shall I do with this extra **ice cream** cone?

I have a good **idea**.

if If means supposing that.

imagination You use your imagination to think of things that are not right in front of you or things that are not real.

If Mr. Snuffle-upagus had wings, he would be a snuffle-bird.

Big Bird has a good **imagination.**

immediately Immediately means right now.

*Operator? Get me the Mudman **immediately**! I'm out of mud.*

important When something is important, it matters very much to someone.

*Mud is **important.***

*Counting is **important.***

*Clues are **important.***

impossible When something is impossible, it cannot be done.

I would like a peanut butter sandwich without any bread.

*That is **impossible,** sir! You cannot make a sandwich without bread.*

in In means within or surrounded by. In means not out.

Little Bird is **in** his nest.

Cookie Monster has his hand **in** the cookie jar.

inch An inch is an amount of distance. There are twelve inches in a foot.

*The six of us together are an **inch** long.*

1 in.

insect An insect is a tiny animal with six legs. Some insects have wings. Some do not.

Butterfly

Ant

Ladybug

Dragonfly

*My favorite **insect** is the ladybug.*

inside   Inside means within.

instead   Instead means in place of.

I am hiding inside Mumphie's hat.

instead   Instead means in place of.

I, the Amazing Mumford, will now pull from this perfectly empty hat a beautiful silk scarf.

A LA PEANUT BUTTER SANDWICHES!

*That's strange! I pulled out a rabbit **instead** of a scarf.*

interesting   When something is interesting, it holds your attention.

*That's an **interesting** rock, Bert.*

Yes, it has many beautiful colors in it, Ernie.

*Gee, Bert. I just thought it was **interesting** because there's a great big spider crawling on it.*

into   When you go into something, you enter it.

Farmer Grover is driving his tractor **into** the barn.

invisible   When something is invisible, you cannot see it.

*Air is all around you, but it is **invisible.***

invite   When you invite someone, you ask that person to come for a visit or to do something with you.

invitation   An invitation is used to ask someone to a party or a special occasion.

*I will **invite** five guests to Fatatatita's birthday party. Here are the **invitations.** Let me count them.... 1, 2, 3, 4, 5! Wonderful!*

iron An iron is a tool used to smooth the wrinkles out of clothes. An iron must be heated before it can be used.

Bert is **ironing** his pigeon costume with an **iron**.

is Grover's favorite story **is** about Super Grover.

The ADVENTURES of SUPER GROVER

island An island is a piece of land that is surrounded by water.

Once upon a time Super Grover was flying over a small **island**.

That little boy on the **island** is about to walk into a patch of poison ivy. I must stop him. Down, down, and away!

it It is a word you use when you are talking or thinking about a thing.

Look at all that poison ivy. I will be careful not to step in **it**.

Don't touch **it**! Don't walk in **it**! Don't pick **it**! Don't…

…land in **it**!

Poison ivy will give you an **itch**.

THE END

itch An itch is a feeling that makes you want to scratch your skin.

Super Grover has an **itch**.

I see that an important I word is missing—insult. An insult is something you say that is not kind—such as, turn the page immediately. You are bothering me.

ABCDEFGHI**J**KLMNOPQRSTUVWXYZ

jacket   A jacket is a short coat.

Hey, Ernie. How do you like my nifty new **jacket**?

PIGEON LOVERS' CLUB

jar   A jar is a kind of container that is usually made of glass. It has a large opening at the top.

Oscar keeps his pickles in a **jar.**

PICKLES

job   A job is work that you do. Most people are paid money for doing their jobs.

Hi! My name is Don Music, and my **job** is writing songs.

I'm the Mudman, and my **job** is delivering mud. Oscar is my best customer.

MUD

Jobs that people do

fire fighter

farmer

mail carrier

baker

sculptor

mechanic

pianist

taxi driver

magician

detective

join   When you join things, you put them together.

Let's all **join** hands and make a circle.

join   When you join a group, you become part of it.

If you **join** the Pigeon Lovers' Club, you can wear one of these nifty jackets.

The PIGEON LOVERS' CLUB

joke   A joke is something you say or do that is funny.

Hey, Ernie. Did you take a bath this morning?

No, Bert. Is there one missing? Hee hee!

That's a very funny **joke,** Ernie! Now clean up your mess!

juice   Juice is the liquid that comes out of a fruit or vegetable.

Betty Lou is thirsty. She is drinking a glass of orange **juice.**

glug
glug

jump   When you jump, both of your feet leave the ground at the same time.

Who can **jump** higher than a house — Grover or Herry Monster?

Both of us can! Houses can't **jump.**

jungle   A jungle is a place full of trees and vines. A jungle is usually warm and damp.

Do you know why I love the **jungle**? The **jungle** is full of interesting animals to count. 1, 2, 3, 4...four interesting animals!

junk   Junk is old or broken things that are usually thrown away.

Ernie! Look at this **junk** in your closet.

That's not **junk,** Bert. I wouldn't throw away my old sneakers, my special autographed footballs, and my favorite broken slinky toy.

Gee, Bert. You have a lot of **junk** in *your* closet, too.

How can you call that **junk**? I would never throw away my collections of bottle caps and wax bananas and paper clips and telephone books.

WAX BANANAS

PAPER CLIPS

BOTTLE CAPS

1956
1955

just   Just means only.

The monster race was **just** for monsters.

just   Just can also mean a very little while ago.

Cookie Monster **just** won the monster race.

just   Just can also mean closely.

Herry Monster came in **just** behind Cookie.

FINISH

The word junk is in this dictionary, but where is the word junkyard? The junkyard is one of my favorite places to visit.

Can you find 8 animals
hidden in the jungle?

Here come the **K**s!

A Silly **K** Poem

A **kangaroo** named **Kathy**
Came hopping into town.
She brought along her **kid**
Whom she dressed up all in brown.
She **kept** him in her pocket,
Which she locked up with a **key**,
But every night she took him out
And **kissed** him 1, 2, 3.

Kk

A B C D E F G H I J **K** L M N O P Q R S T U V W X Y Z

kangaroo   A kangaroo is an animal that has strong back legs for jumping. A mother kangaroo carries her baby in a pouch.

I am a baby **kangaroo.** I am a joey.

We are the joey's mother and father. We are **kangaroos.**

keep   When you keep something, you have it.
Sometimes you hold it and sometimes you put it in a special place.

Ernie! Why are all of your marbles in the cookie jar?

That's where I **keep** my marble collection.

Then where are you **keeping** the cookies I made this morning?

I'm **keeping** them in a special place.

What special place?

My stomach!

keep   When you keep doing something, you go on doing it.

As long as the sheep **keep** jumping, I will **keep** counting them. 108, 109, 110…

key A key is something that is used to open a lock.

keyhole A keyhole is an opening for a key.

The castle door was locked. Prince Charming put the **key** into the **keyhole.**

Prince Charming

kick When you kick something, you hit it with your foot.

Ernie likes to **kick** his football.

Farmer Grover's cow **kicked** over the milk pail.

kid Kid means young goat. In everyday talk, kid is used to mean child.

Did you know that a **kid** can be a young goat or a child?

You're **kidding**!

Someone who is **kidding** is joking.

KID
KID

kill When you kill something, you make it die.

Wow, I can **kill** seven in one blow!

The little tailor **killed** seven flies with a fly swatter.

kind When you are kind, you are friendly and helpful.

Big Bird dropped his groceries. Betty Lou helped him pick them up. That was a **kind** thing to do.

kind Kind also means sort or type.

> What **kind** of sandwich would you like, sir?

> I'll have a peanut butter and jelly sandwich.

> What **kind** of peanut butter — crunchy or plain? What **kind** of jelly — grape or gooseberry? What **kind** of bread …

> This is ridiculous! Just bring me an ordinary peanut butter and jelly sandwich on a plate.

> Very well, sir! What **kind** of plate?

kindergarten Kindergarten is the class at school that comes before first grade.

Farley is helping the **kindergarten** teacher. He is passing out the scissors and paste.

king A king is a man who rules a country.

King Cookie is sitting on his throne.

> Me proclaim today National Cookie Day!

kiss When you kiss, you touch a person with your lips. A kiss shows love or friendship.

Betty Lou is going to **kiss** Grover.

kitchen A kitchen is a room where food is cooked.

Bert is in the **kitchen** cooking oatmeal.

kite A kite is a toy made of paper, plastic, or wood. It flies in the air on the end of a long string.

Big Bird is flying a **kite.**

kitten A kitten is a young cat.

My cat, Fatatatita, has **kittens.** Not only are they adorable, but I can count them. 1, 2, 3, 4, 5, 6… six **kittens**!

knee The knee is the middle part of your leg. Your leg bends at the knee. Look up the word body.

Betty Lou has a bandage on her **knee.**

knife A knife is a tool that is used to cut things. It has a handle and a blade.

Waiter! This **knife** does not cut very well. Please bring me something a little sharper.

Right away, sir!

knock   When you knock, you hit your knuckles against something to make a noise.

Herry Monster is going to **knock** on Betty Lou's door.

Next time, Herry, don't **knock**. Use the doorbell.

knot   A knot is made by tying together pieces of one or more ropes, ribbons, or strings.

I, the Count, am tied up with ropes. Will I escape? Of course! But, first, let me count the **knots** in the ropes! 1 **knot**, 2 **knots**. Isn't this fun? 3 **knots**, 4 **knots**...

know   When you know something, you are sure of it.

My address is 123 Sesame Street.

Farley **knows** his address.

koala   A koala is a small furry animal with big ears and no tail. A koala looks like a little bear, but it is not a bear.

Koalas live in eucalyptus trees and are very shy.

KEEP OUT!
KEEP OFF!
KEEP AWAY!
KEEP QUIET!

Keep is my favorite word that begins with K. Can you guess why?

THE H.I.J.K GAME!

One of the things in each group doesn't belong. Can you find it?